Little Guides to
Great Lives

CHARLES DARWIN

LAURENCE KING

Published in 2018
by Laurence King Publishing Ltd
361–373 City Road
London EC1V 1LR
United Kingdom
Tel: +44 20 7841 6900
E-mail: enquiries@laurenceking.com
www.laurenceking.com

A catalog record for this book is available
from the British Library

ISBN: 978-1-78627-295-9

Commissioning Editor: Chloë Pursey
Editor: Leah Willey
Design concept: Charlotte Bolton
Designer: Stuart Dando

Printed in China

Little Guides to
Great Lives

CHARLES
DARWIN

Written by
Dan Green

Illustrations by
Rachel Katstaller

Laurence King Publishing

Charles Darwin is famous for his <u>theory</u> of <u>evolution</u> by natural selection—a theory that helps us explain life on Earth.

Charles' idea that living things change over time and <u>adapt</u> to the place where they live is one of the most important discoveries in science. In the 1800s and 1900s, it changed the way people thought about the world.

The theory of evolution by natural selection did not come to Charles in one "lightbulb moment." It was the result of many decades of patient work, building on the ideas of scientists who had gone before him.

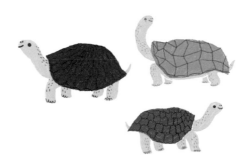

As he was growing up, no one would have guessed that young Charles was going to change the world. He was born in 1809 into a large and wealthy family. The Darwins lived in Shrewsbury, England, in a big house called the Mount.

Erasmus
(Grandad)

Mary
(Grandma)

Susannah
(Mother)

Marianne   Susan   Caroline   Emily
Catherine

Charles grew up with four sisters and a brother.
Like every other rich boy in nineteenth-century
England, he enjoyed tearing about the countryside,
riding, hunting, birdwatching, and fishing.

Robert
(Father)

Charles

Shelah

Czar

Spark

Erasmus
("Ras")

Charles and his older brother, Ras, were best friends. They set up a <u>chemistry</u> lab in the toolshed, where they blew things up, grew crystals, and created terrible stinks. Charles was often up to mischief and couldn't resist adventures, such as stealing apples and plums from the orchard.

When Charles was eight years old, his mom died. A gloom settled over Robert Darwin, and the fun went out of the Mount. Charles' older sisters had to look after the younger children.

The following year, Charles was sent to a boarding school. It was rules, rules, rules. He hated all the lessons he had to learn, and continued to get up to mischief instead. Charles was happiest when he was alone outdoors.

I loved to go exploring and collecting in the countryside.

The headmaster got cross with Charles for wasting his time outside when he should have been learning Latin and Greek. But Charles was developing a passion for collecting and an eye for detail that would one day help him to understand nature in a brand-new way.

Charles left school at 16. His dad arranged for him to study medicine at Edinburgh University, where Ras was studying too. Once again, Charles was bored stiff. He was also terrified of blood, and ran out of two gruesome lessons before learning anything at all.

In his second year at university, Charles made friends with some people studying <u>geology</u> and <u>zoology</u>. He began going to some of their lessons, but he found these just as dull, preferring to explore nature himself. His dad was not impressed.

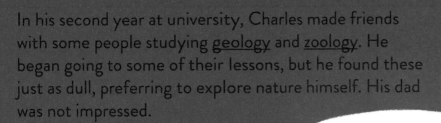

You care for nothing but shooting, dogs, and rat-catching, and you will be a disgrace to yourself and all your family!

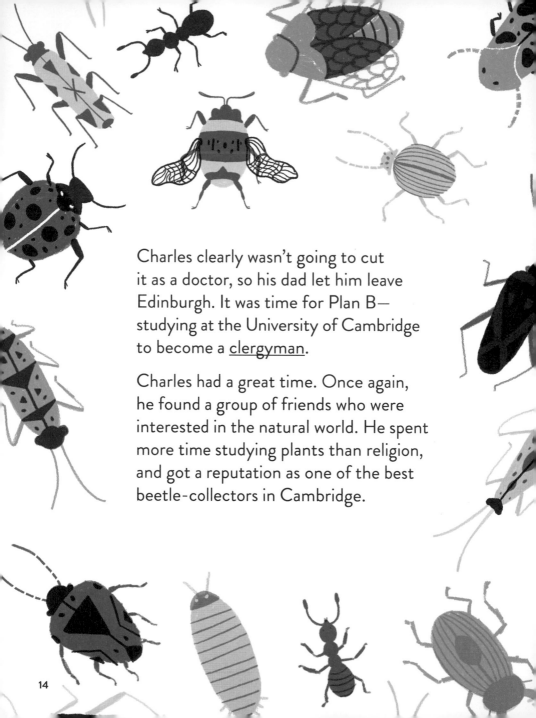

Charles clearly wasn't going to cut
it as a doctor, so his dad let him leave
Edinburgh. It was time for Plan B—
studying at the University of Cambridge
to become a <u>clergyman</u>.

Charles had a great time. Once again,
he found a group of friends who were
interested in the natural world. He spent
more time studying plants than religion,
and got a reputation as one of the best
beetle-collectors in Cambridge.

One day while out "beetling," Charles spotted a beauty hiding under some bark. But he already had a rare beetle in each hand, so he popped one of them into his mouth so he could pick up the third.

To my unspeakable disgust and pain, the little inconsiderate beast squirted acid down my throat!

Charles spat out the beetle and watched in dismay as the third beetle got away too!

Charles passed his exams and finished university. But before he could start life as a vicar, there was an unexpected turn. Coming home after a <u>fossil</u>-hunting trip in Wales, he found a letter from one of his closest friends.

24 August 1831
Cambridge

My dear Darwin,

I have been asked to recommend a <u>naturalist</u> to join Captain FitzRoy on a voyage to <u>survey</u> South America. The job will involve collecting, observing, and noting anything worthy to be noted in Natural History. The voyage is to last two years. Don't be afraid that you are not qualified, for I assure you I think you are the very man they are in search of.

John Stevens Henslow
Professor of <u>Botany</u>
University of Cambridge

Charles' heart leapt at the chance to explore the world, discovering new plants and animals along the way.
The only snag was that his dad thought it was dangerous, expensive, and a complete waste of time.

Luckily, Charles' uncle, Josiah Wedgwood, persuaded Robert Darwin that the voyage could be good for Charles.

The voyage would be the biggest event of Charles'
life, but first he had to meet Captain FitzRoy. The
meeting seemed to go well. It was only later that
Charles found out he almost lost the job because of
the shape of his nose!

When everything was agreed, Charles rushed around buying equipment for the two-year voyage:

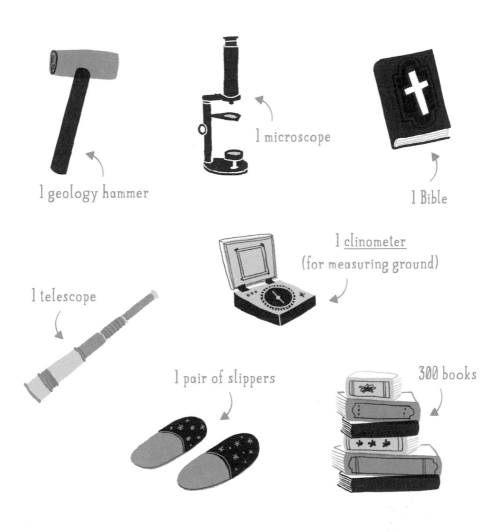

1 microscope

1 geology hammer

1 Bible

1 clinometer
(for measuring ground)

1 telescope

1 pair of slippers

300 books

Little did Charles know, it would actually be five years before he returned to England.

When Charles saw HMS *Beagle* for the first time, he was amazed at how small the ship was. Sixty-five crew members and nine passengers would soon be crammed onboard.

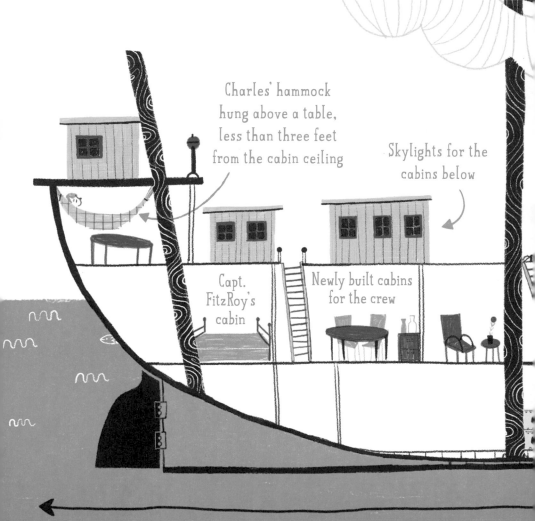

Charles' hammock hung above a table, less than three feet from the cabin ceiling

Skylights for the cabins below

Capt. FitzRoy's cabin

Newly built cabins for the crew

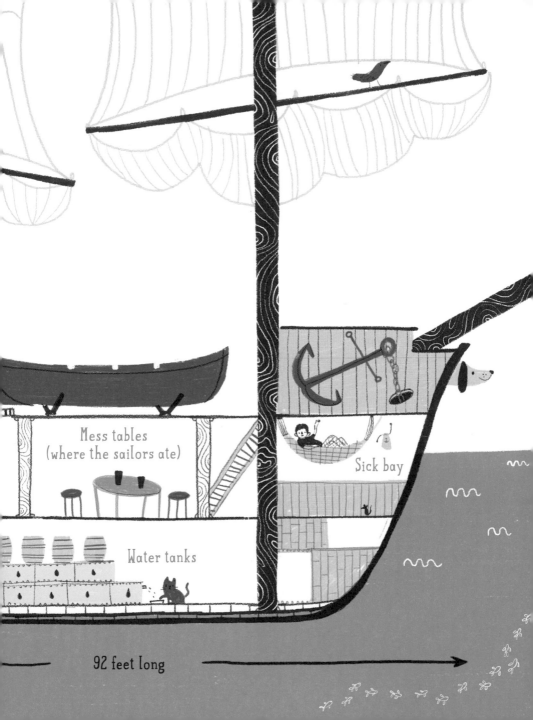

Mess tables
(where the sailors ate)

Sick bay

Water tanks

92 feet long

On 27 December 1831, HMS *Beagle* finally set sail.
Even though Charles was often seasick, he enjoyed
living on the ship. He kept a diary for the entire
voyage, as well as writing hundreds of pages of
notes and letters.

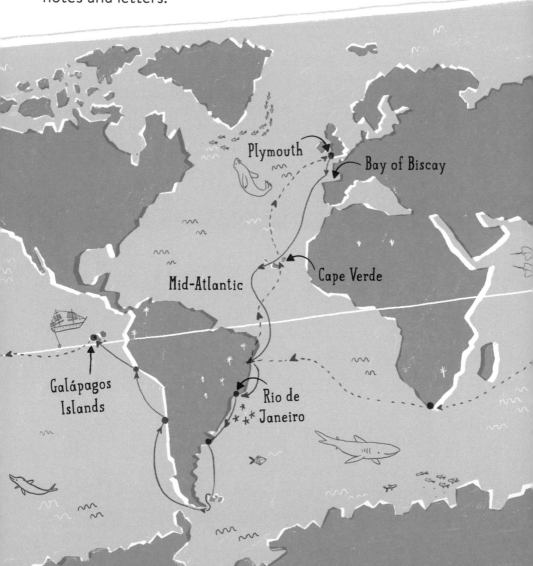

Plymouth

Bay of Biscay

Mid-Atlantic

Cape Verde

Galápagos
Islands

Rio de
Janeiro

Plymouth, Dec 1831
These two months in Plymouth were the most miserable which I ever spent.

Bay of Biscay, Dec 1831
I found the only thing my stomach would bear was biscuit and raisins.

1831–1835, England to Galápagos Islands

1835–1836, Galápagos Islands back to England (via Australia)

Cape Verde, Jan 1832
Collecting loads of amazing octopuses. Why would God put so much beauty out here, where there is no one to see it?

Mid-Atlantic, Feb 1832
I find a ship a very comfortable house... if it was not for seasickness the whole world would be sailors.

Equator

Australia

Equator, Feb 1832
Those that have never crossed the Equator are dunked, shaved, and treated roughly. Great fun.

Rio, June 1832
I am red-hot with spiders!

N
W E
S

Almost every stop on the journey left Charles amazed, as he crammed his head (and the ship) full of plants and animals he'd never seen before. He planned to make his name as a scientist by discovering as many new <u>species</u> as possible.

Charles made a net to drag behind the ship, to catch sea creatures, and on land he dug for fossils. In South America, he hauled the skull of a giant armadillo on to the ship.

In Argentina, Charles went on an expedition, riding across the plains with gauchos (cowboys). He had heard about a rare bird called a rhea and he wanted to find it, but he couldn't spot one anywhere.

Then one dinnertime, he realized he had been tucking into just such a bird! Darwin saved the bones and feathers and pieced it back together.

After rounding the tip of South America, HMS *Beagle* made its way up the coast of Chile in early 1835. Here Charles saw two things that rocked his world—quite literally!

First he saw a volcanic eruption, as Mount Osorno spurted out rock and volcanic ash.

Then, when he was visiting the town of Valdivia, a huge earthquake struck.

Charles was amazed at Earth's raw power. He found that the earthquake had moved huge chunks of land. If all this could happen in just a few minutes, what changes might have happened to our planet over thousands or even millions of years?

In September 1835, HMS *Beagle* arrived at the Galápagos Islands. At first, Charles was not a fan of the 13 small, sun-baked volcanic islands, calling them "black, dismal-looking heaps of broken lava." The black sand was as hot as a stove and painful to walk on.

However, Charles was soon impressed by the variety of species he found on the islands, including animals that were found nowhere else on Earth.

He was curious about how the creatures came to be on these remote islands in the first place. Charles busied himself mapping the islands and collecting more <u>specimens</u> to take back home.

Charles noticed that the plants and animals looked a bit like those he had seen on the mainland, but with some important differences. Even between the individual islands, Charles could spot differences.

Some of the oddest inhabitants were the enormous tortoises. These lumbering giants were large enough to ride and they hissed when anyone got too close to them!

The governor of the Galápagos Islands told Charles that he could tell which island a tortoise came from just by looking at the shape of its shell.

Hood Island

Isabela Island

Pinta Island

This got Charles thinking, and for the last two years of his voyage he wondered about the <u>origins</u> of these various species. But it wouldn't be until he got home that he would realize just how important these differences were.

After five years at sea, Charles was delighted to finally return to England. He arrived back at the Mount in the middle of the night on 4 October 1836. The next morning he gave his family the surprise of their lives at breakfast!

Over the next two years, Charles toured the country speaking and writing about his adventures. He also began thinking about the future and decided that he needed a wife. Even marriage was treated like a scientific problem, with Charles listing the pros and cons.

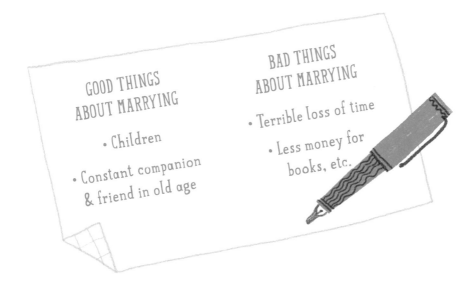

GOOD THINGS ABOUT MARRYING

- Children
- Constant companion & friend in old age

BAD THINGS ABOUT MARRYING

- Terrible loss of time
- Less money for books, etc.

Eventually, Charles decided it was a good idea to propose to his cousin, Emma Wedgwood. They were married in January 1839.

Charles was becoming famous for all the fantastic fossils and specimens he'd collected on the *Beagle* voyage. There were 1,529 bottled species and 3,907 labeled specimens, so it took Charles and his friends years to sort and catalog them all! In 1845, he collected his tales of adventure into a book, which was a big hit.

Full title: *A Naturalist's Voyage; Journal of researches into the natural history and geology of the countries visited during the voyage of H.M.S. Beagle round the world, under the command of Captain FitzRoy, R.N.*

Snappy title!

But Charles wasn't satisfied with writing about his adventures. His mind was still buzzing with unanswered questions about the things he had seen on his long voyage. How did all those different species of plants and animals come to be on the planet? This is what Charles would later call the "mystery of mysteries."

That armadillo skull I collected in South America looks like a massive version of today's anteaters and armadillos. Why has one been replaced by the other over time?

That rhea I discovered (on my plate!) is not the only kind of rhea living in South America.

Why are there two species of rhea living so close to each other?

Charles was interested in theories of evolution—the idea that species of plants and animals were not fixed, but could change over time.

Evolution was not a new idea. Many scientists already agreed that species do change over time—fossils of <u>extinct</u> creatures were <u>evidence</u> of this. However, they did not agree about HOW this change happened.

One of the most popular ideas about how evolution happened had been put forward by French scientist Jean-Baptiste de Lamarck in the early 1800s. He imagined that living things developed the features and behaviors that they used most, and passed these changes on to their young.

Lamarck's theory tried to explain how giraffes developed long necks. His idea went something like this...

In ancient times, giraffes with short necks strained to reach the juicy leaves on high branches.

As they stretched up, their necks got a little longer.

They then passed this improved, longer neck on to their young.

Theories like this weren't correct, but they did get Charles thinking about what was really going on.

Charles had a lot to think about, but his life was also full of distractions—he had a big family to look after now and worries about his own health. He decided to move out of smoky, dirty London to a big house in the countryside called Down House. The huge garden became Charles' laboratory.

Charles took up gardening and pigeon-breeding. He built a long pathway so he could take a daily walk while he was thinking, and he exchanged letters with hundreds of people around the world. In his mind, he traveled back to the Galápagos Islands, over and over again.

Pigeon-breeding let Charles see firsthand how flexible life can be. Starting with dull-looking wild pigeons, breeders had created dozens of flamboyant varieties. They did this by picking wild pigeons with particular features, and breeding them.

Big eyes

Frilly feathers

Tail feathers
like a peacock

Puff-up-able
throat

Feathery
feet

The fabulous features were passed on to the pigeons' <u>offspring</u>, and the process was repeated over and over again. This is called <u>artificial</u> selection.

As Charles saw the process of artificial selection in pigeon-breeding, things began to fall into place. He realized that a similar process also happens in nature, and his theory of evolution through natural selection finally came together. The theory goes something like this:

1. Life is a struggle for survival

Most living things produce far more offspring than can survive long enough to have offspring of their own.

2. Variation

Members of a species are not exactly the same—there are lots of small differences between them. Natural variation means that some individuals will be better suited to their environment than others.

3. Natural selection

The individuals that are best suited to their environment are the ones most likely to survive long enough to have offspring of their own.

4. Features are inherited from parents

The individuals that survive long enough to reproduce will pass on their "winning" features to their offspring.

5. Adaptation

Over time, more of the individuals in a group will be born with those "winning" features. This makes the group better adapted to their surroundings.

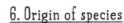

6. Origin of species

When a group of living things becomes very different from the original group, a new species has appeared.

All these ideas were already out there. Charles' breakthrough was to connect them together.

Charles had cracked it! But there was a big problem. He worried that his theory would be rejected by Victorian society, especially by people like his wife Emma, who believed that all the plants and animals on Earth had been made the way they were by God. Although he shared his theory with some of his friends, he didn't publish his ideas in a book.

Writing these ideas down feels like confessing to a murder.

Perhaps I should just write a big book about barnacles instead...*

*He did!

Then, in 1858, everything changed. Charles received a letter from a young naturalist called Alfred Russel Wallace. Inside was a theory about evolution!

It was so similar to Charles' own theory, it was as though Alfred had read Charles' innermost thoughts. Charles felt sick with despair. If Alfred published these ideas before him, Charles' years of work would be wasted!

Charles' friends persuaded him to write a short essay of his own, and both his and Wallace's theories were read out at a meeting in London in July 1858.

With the theory now out in public, there was no time to waste. Charles kicked into high gear and cranked out a whole book in a year.

Inside, Charles wrote about his big idea using simple language that everyone could understand. The first part of the book explained Charles' theory of evolution by natural selection and the rest of the book set out the huge amount of evidence he had collected over decades, from his discoveries aboard HMS *Beagle* to things he had spotted in his own garden.

The book that would change the world was published in 1859.

On the Origin
of Species by
Means of Natural
Selection

On the Origin of Species was an instant hit, and it sold out on the very first day.

Not everyone was happy with what they had read in Charles' book. Although Charles had not actually mentioned human evolution, many people thought his ideas meant that humans were <u>descended</u> from apes. People were furious and arguments about the book raged up and down the country. One of the biggest took place on the evening of 30 June 1860.

I am sharpening up my claws and beak in readiness!

IN ONE CORNER, bringing the fight for the theory of evolution by natural selection, was Thomas Huxley— a.k.a. "Darwin's bulldog."

One thousand people crammed into a hall at the University of Oxford to watch the "Great Debate." The crowd booed and jeered, cheered, and waved their hankies. One person even fainted.

IN THE OTHER CORNER, defending the idea that species do NOT change, was the Bishop of Oxford, Samuel Wilberforce.

Are you descended from an ape on your mom or dad's side?

In the end, both sides claimed victory, and they all went cheerfully off to dinner together.

Charles' book fired up strong feelings because people liked the idea that humans had a special place in nature. Many thought that if humans had evolved through natural selection, they must be no different from other creatures.

Does this mean I'm related to apes? What rot!

Surely people aren't the same as common beasts!

Darwin is the most dangerous man in England!

Despite all of the arguments, many scientists were enthusiastic about Charles' theory, because it had the potential to explain so much of what we see around us. In just a decade, many ordinary people and even some religious leaders began to accept Charles' ideas.

Charles was now world-famous and the proud owner of the most magnificent beard in science. He didn't really like the attention, preferring to stay at home writing books about nature. These included an important book on orchids and a masterpiece on the lives of earthworms.

In 1871, after collecting more evidence and being encouraged by some of the positive reactions to his theory, Charles published another book.

This time, he bravely applied his theory of evolution to humans, arguing that humans, gorillas, chimpanzees, and orangutans evolved simultaneously from a common <u>ancestor</u>. *The Descent of Man* was a hit. People were now less shocked by the idea of evolution. It later turned out that some of Charles' ideas weren't quite right, but he still kickstarted several new branches of science.

Charles Darwin died in 1882, aged 73. He was honored with a burial in London's Westminster Abbey, close to Isaac Newton (another super-famous scientist).

Since his death, Charles has become even more famous and his name is remembered around the world...

...in the names of animals...

Darwin's frog

Darwin's finch

...in place names...

Mount Darwin
in South America

...and even in space.

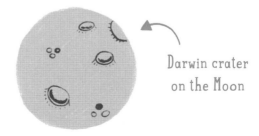

Darwin crater
on the Moon

Charles is a towering figure in the history of science. His power was learning to look at things closely, and his natural curiosity about the world kept him asking questions. Most importantly, he wasn't afraid to be honest about what he saw, even if it led him to radical conclusions.

There is grandeur in this view of life...from so simple a beginning, endless forms most beautiful and most wonderful have been, and are being, evolved.

LIFE AFTER DARWIN

After Darwin's death, more and more
evidence for evolution by natural
selection came to light. Many new
discoveries in the twentieth century
helped to explain things that Charles
had not been able to figure out. For
example, it had once been argued that
Earth was too young for living things
to have evolved slowly, through the
gradual <u>accumulation</u> of tiny changes.
The discovery that Earth is actually
around 4.5 billion years old showed
that there had been plenty of time
for natural selection to produce the
range of life we see today.

Hundreds of new fossil discoveries
also provided some of the "missing
links" in the story of evolution. As
Charles had predicted, they showed
that humans and the other apes
evolved from a common ancestor. And
if we go back even further we can find
ancestors shared by all amphibians,
birds, reptiles, and mammals.

Gaps in the evolutionary record are still being filled more than 150 years later. Tiktaalik was found in 2004. This strange creature lived 375 million years ago. It lived in the water, but had a mixture of ocean-going and land-going features. Scientists think it could teach us about the evolutionary transition from fish to amphibians.

Genetics

When he wrote *On the Origin of Species*, Charles didn't know how variation between individuals arose. The science of <u>genetics</u> provided an answer.

Variation is caused by differences in genes inside the cells of living things. Offspring get a random selection of genes from their mother and father, producing a wide variety of different combinations. Sometimes bigger differences arise due to mutations— random chemical changes in genes.

Scientists are still busy studying genes today—who knows what amazing discoveries they'll make next!

Genes are found inside nearly every <u>cell</u> of living things, encoded in a chemical called DNA.

TIMELINE

1809
Charles Darwin is born in Shrewsbury, England, on 12 February.

1817
Charles' mother dies and he is looked after by his older sisters.

1818
Charles is sent to a boarding school in Shrewsbury.

1831
Charles is told about an opportunity aboard HMS *Beagle*.

The ship departs and Charles begins his five-year voyage.

1832
HMS *Beagle* visits Tenerife, Cape Verde, Brazil, Argentina, and Tierra del Fuego.

1833
HMS *Beagle* visits the Falkland Islands.

Throughout the voyage, Charles makes notes and collects plant and animal specimens.

1837–8
Charles begins thinking about evolution and puzzling over the origin of species.

1839
Charles marries Emma Wedgwood.

1842
Charles moves out of London to Down House in Kent.

1860
Discussion about Charles' book takes place up and down the country.

1871
The Descent of Man is published. In this book, Charles applies his theory of evolution to humans.

1882
Charles dies on 19 April, aged 73.

1825

Charles' dad enrols him at Edinburgh University to study medicine.

1827

Charles quits medical school and begins studying theology at the University of Cambridge.

1828

Preferring to study the natural world, Charles starts attending botany classes and becomes an excellent beetle-collector.

1834

HMS *Beagle* sails around Cape Horn (the tip of South America) and towards the coast of Chile.

1835

Charles spends five weeks exploring the Galápagos Islands.

1836

After visiting Australia, HMS *Beagle* sails around the Cape of Good Hope (in South Africa), returns to Brazil, and then finally arrives back in England.

1840s–1850s

Gradually, Charles' theory of evolution by natural selection falls into place. He starts writing down his ideas, but he doesn't publish them.

1858

Alfred Russel Wallace sends Charles a theory about evolution which is shockingly similar to Charles' own ideas. Both theories are read out at a meeting in London.

1859

On the Origin of Species by Means of Natural Selection is published.

Today

Since Charles' death, new evidence has been found to support his theory of evolution by natural selection.

Charles Darwin is one of the most famous scientists of all time, remembered for his attention to detail and his limitless curiosity about the natural world.

Charles Darwin

GLOSSARY

accumulation – a collection, usually made over a long stretch of time.

adapt – to change in order to better suit the surrounding environment.

ancestor – an early species of animal or plant from which a new species has evolved. Ancestors can also be close relatives (e.g., your parents, grandparents, or great-grandparents).

artificial – a process or object that is made or affected by humans (not naturally occurring).

botany – the study of plants.

cell – the smallest part of a living thing. Most animals and plants are made up of millions of cells.

chemistry – the study of matter, things such as atoms, gases and elements, and how they interact with each other.

clergyman – a leading member of a church or religious group.

clinometer – a piece of equipment used for measuring land (especially slopes or hills).

descended – to be related to (e.g., you are descended from your parents, grandparents, great-grandparents, etc.).

Equator – an imaginary line that goes around the middle of Earth.

evidence – information that is used to prove that a theory is correct.

evolution – the process in which species of plants and animals gradually change over time.

extinct – when a species of plant or animal has died out and there are no longer any living members.

fossil – the preserved remains of plants and animals from thousands of years ago.

genetics – the study of how features and characteristics are passed from one generation to the next through genes. A gene is a part of the DNA in a plant or animal that is inherited from the previous generation and carries the information about individual characteristics.

geology – the study, through the examination of rock and soil, of Earth's structure and how it changes over time.

naturalist – a person who studies the natural world, including plants and animals.

offspring – the children or young of a parent.

origins – where something has come from.

species – a particular group of plants or animals that share characteristics.

specimen – a plant or animal that is examined by scientists and used as an example of a whole species.

survey – to examine and measure land, often in order to make a map.

theory – an idea that tries to explain something.

zoology – the study of animals.

INDEX

CREDITS

Photograph of Charles Darwin on page 61 courtesy of Library of Congress, Prints and Photographs Division, Washington, D.C.